NOVENA TO

ST. KATERI TEKAKWITHA

A 9-Day Journey of Faith and Prayer

REV MARK C TILLEY

NOVENA TO ST. KATERI TEKAKWITHA

Copyright © 2024 By Rev MARK C TILLEY

All rights reserved. No part of this publication may be reproduced, stored or transmitted in any form or by any means, electronic, mechanical, photocopying, recording, scanning, or otherwise without written permission from the publisher. It is illegal to copy this book, post it to a website, or distribute it by any other means without permission.

TABLE OF CONTENTS

INTRODUCTION... 4
BIOGRAPHY OF ST. KATERI TEKAKWITHA...7
LEGACY OF ST. KATERI TEKAKWITHA........11
DAY 1 – ST. KATERI TEKAKWITHA.................14
DAY 2 – ST. KATERI TEKAKWITHA.................17
DAY 3 – ST. KATERI TEKAKWITHA.................20
DAY 4 – ST. KATERI TEKAKWITHA.................23
DAY 5 – ST. KATERI TEKAKWITHA.................26
DAY 6 – ST. KATERI TEKAKWITHA.................29
DAY 7 – ST. KATERI TEKAKWITHA.................32
DAY 8 – ST. KATERI TEKAKWITHA.................35
DAY 9 – ST. KATERI TEKAKWITHA.................38
GRATITUDE PRAYER FOR ANSWERED
PRAYER... 41
CONCLUSION..43

INTRODUCTION

Welcome to a journey of faith and inspiration with the Novena to St. Kateri Tekakwitha, affectionately known as the Lily of the Mohawks.

Imagine stepping into the world of a remarkable soul whose life was a tapestry of love, humility, and unwavering dedication to God and others.

St. Kateri's story isn't just history; it's a living testament to the power of faith and the beauty of a life transformed by grace.

As we embark on these nine days of prayer and reflection, we invite you to join us in seeking St. Kateri's intercession for [mention your intention].

Her virtues—her deep love for God, her gentle spirit of sacrifice, her steadfast courage in the face of adversity—speak to us across centuries, touching our hearts with their timeless relevance.

Throughout this novena, we'll explore how St. Kateri's devotion to the Holy Eucharist fueled her spiritual journey. Her love for the Mass and frequent reception of Communion were not mere rituals but profound encounters with Christ's presence. It's a reminder that our faith isn't just about words but about experiencing God's love in tangible ways, just as she did.

Together, let's pray with hope and expectation, asking St. Kateri to walk alongside us in our daily struggles and joys. May her prayers help us avoid sin, grow in holiness, and find true peace in God's plan for our lives. This novena isn't just about the past; it's about renewing our faith today, drawing inspiration from St. Kateri's journey to enrich our own.

Join us as we delve into her inspiring life, allowing her example to ignite our hearts with a deeper love for God and a stronger desire to live authentically as followers of Christ. Let's discover together how St. Kateri's story can resonate with our own, guiding us toward a life filled with grace, purpose, and enduring hope.

BIOGRAPHY OF ST. KATERI TEKAKWITHA

St. Kateri Tekakwitha, known as the Lily of the Mohawks, was born in 1656 in the Mohawk village of Ossernenon, near present-day Auriesville, New York. Her mother was an Algonquin, taken captive by the Mohawks and married to a Mohawk chief. Her father was a Mohawk warrior.

From an early age, Kateri faced adversity and loss—her parents and younger brother perished in a smallpox epidemic that also left her physically frail and with impaired eyesight.

Despite these hardships, Kateri's spirit remained resilient. Raised in the Mohawk tradition, she was known for her gentleness, kindness, and deep love for nature.

Her life took a profound turn when she encountered Jesuit missionaries who visited her village. Through their teachings, Kateri became captivated by the Christian faith. She was baptized on Easter Sunday in 1676, at the age of twenty, taking the name Kateri, a form of Catherine in honor of St. Catherine of Siena.

Kateri's decision to embrace Christianity was met with hostility and persecution from her own people, who viewed her conversion as a betrayal of their traditions. Despite the challenges and ostracism she faced, Kateri remained steadfast in her faith. She fled to the Christian Native community of Kahnawake near Montreal, Canada, where she lived a life of prayer, penance, and devotion.

In Kahnawake, Kateri devoted herself to a life of intense prayer and service to others, caring for the sick and elderly.

She was known for her deep love for the Holy Eucharist, often spending hours in prayer before the Blessed Sacrament. Her humility, simplicity, and purity of heart inspired those around her, drawing many to the Christian faith.

Throughout her life, Kateri endured physical suffering and illness, but she embraced her trials as opportunities to unite herself more closely with Christ's Passion. She died on April 17, 1680, at the age of twenty-four. Witness accounts describe her face radiating with peace and serenity at the moment of her death.

St. Kateri Tekakwitha was beatified by Pope John Paul II in 1980 and canonized by Pope Benedict XVI on October 21, 2012. She is the first Native American saint and is revered as a model of virtue and holiness. Her feast day is celebrated on July 14th in the Roman Catholic Church.

St. Kateri Tekakwitha's life continues to inspire millions around the world, especially those facing adversity and seeking spiritual strength. Her example of courage, faith, and unwavering love for God serves as a beacon of hope and encouragement for all who strive to live a life of holiness and virtue.

LEGACY OF ST. KATERI TEKAKWITHA

Imagine a young woman, born into a world of deep traditions and profound spirituality among the Mohawk people in 17th-century America.

This was Kateri Tekakwitha—known for her gentleness, kindness, and unwavering spirit. Her life, though brief, left an indelible mark on history, inspiring generations with her faith, courage, and love.

Kateri's journey to Christianity was one of personal conviction and courage. Despite facing rejection and persecution from her own community, she embraced the Catholic faith, finding solace and strength in Christ's teachings. Her baptism marked a profound turning point, not just for her personally, but as a symbol of reconciliation between her Indigenous heritage and newfound faith—a testament to unity amidst cultural diversity.

At the heart of Kateri's devotion was her love for the Holy Eucharist. She cherished the Mass as a sacred encounter with Christ, spending hours in prayer before the Blessed Sacrament. Her deep spiritual connection serves as a reminder of the transformative power of faith and communion with God—a lesson that continues to resonate deeply in today's world.

Beyond her spiritual journey, Kateri lived a life of service and compassion. In Kahnawake, she cared for the sick and elderly with tenderness and humility, embodying Christ's love in practical acts of kindness. Her example teaches us that holiness is found not in grand gestures, but in everyday acts of love and mercy towards others.

St. Kateri Tekakwitha's canonization in 2012 as the first Native American saint was a moment of joy and celebration for the faithful worldwide.

Her story transcends cultural boundaries, inspiring diverse communities to embrace faith, justice, and mutual respect. Her feast day on July 14th is a time of reverence and gratitude, honoring her life and seeking her intercession in prayers for healing and peace.

Today, Kateri's legacy lives on in schools, hospitals, and social services that bear her name—testaments to her enduring influence in promoting education, healthcare, and social justice. Her life challenges us to embrace our differences, cultivate compassion, and live lives rooted in faith and service to others.

St. Kateri Tekakwitha's story continues to touch hearts and souls, reminding us of the power of faith to overcome adversity and unite diverse cultures in a shared journey towards love and grace. Her legacy invites us all to walk with courage, kindness, and a steadfast trust in God's boundless mercy.

DAY 1 – ST. KATERI TEKAKWITHA

In the name of the Father, and of the Son, and of the Holy Spirit. Amen.

St. Kateri Tekakwitha, beloved child and Lily of the Mohawks, I come before you seeking your intercession for [mention your request here].

I am inspired by the virtues that graced your soul: your deep love for God and neighbor, your humility, obedience, patience, purity, and your spirit of sacrifice. Help me to emulate these virtues in my own life. Through God's abundant grace, which led you to the true faith and holiness, intercede for me and guide me.

DAILY REFLECTION:

Today, contemplate on the virtue of obedience that St. Kateri practiced in her life. Obedience to God's will leads us closer to Him and brings about His blessings.

BIBLE PASSAGE: "If you love me, you will obey my commandments." - John 14:15 (GNT)

Grant me a fervent devotion to the Holy Eucharist, that I may cherish Holy Mass as you did and receive Holy Communion frequently. Teach me to embrace the Cross of our crucified Savior joyfully, as you did, so that I may carry my daily burdens with love for Him who suffered for me. Above all, pray that I may avoid sin, lead a life of holiness, and attain salvation.

Amen.

St. Kateri Tekakwitha, pray for us.

NOVENA TO ST. KATERI TEKAKWITHA

RECITE THESE:

Our Father…
Hail Mary…
 Glory Be…

DAY 2 – ST. KATERI TEKAKWITHA

In the name of the Father, and of the Son, and of the Holy Spirit. Amen.

St. Kateri Tekakwitha, beloved child and Lily of the Mohawks, I come before you seeking your intercession for [mention your request here].

I am inspired by the virtues that graced your soul: your deep love for God and neighbor, your humility, obedience, patience, purity, and your spirit of sacrifice. Help me to emulate these virtues in my own life. Through God's abundant grace, which led you to the true faith and holiness, intercede for me and guide me.

DAILY REFLECTION:

Today, reflect on St. Kateri's patience in suffering. She endured hardships with unwavering faith and trust in God's providence.

BIBLE PASSAGE: "But if we hope for what we do not yet have, we wait for it patiently." - Romans 8:25 (GNT)

Grant me a fervent devotion to the Holy Eucharist, that I may cherish Holy Mass as you did and receive Holy Communion frequently. Teach me to love our crucified Savior as deeply as you did, so that I may joyfully carry my daily crosses for love of Him who suffered for me. Above all, pray that I may avoid sin, lead a life of holiness, and attain eternal salvation.

Amen.

St. Kateri Tekakwitha, pray for us.

NOVENA TO ST. KATERI TEKAKWITHA

RECITE THESE:

Our Father…
Hail Mary…
Glory Be…

DAY 3 – ST. KATERI TEKAKWITHA

In the name of the Father, and of the Son, and of the Holy Spirit. Amen.

St. Kateri Tekakwitha, beloved child and Lily of the Mohawks, I come before you seeking your intercession for [mention your request here].

I am inspired by the virtues that graced your soul: your deep love for God and neighbor, your humility, obedience, patience, purity, and your spirit of sacrifice. Help me to emulate these virtues in my own life. Through God's abundant grace, which led you to the true faith and holiness, intercede for me and guide me.

DAILY REFLECTION:

Today, reflect on St. Kateri's love for God and neighbor. She exemplified selfless love and dedication to serving others.

BIBLE PASSAGE: "Love the Lord your God with all your heart, with all your soul, and with all your mind." - **Matthew 22:37 (GNT)**

Grant me a fervent devotion to the Holy Eucharist, so that I may cherish Holy Mass as you did and receive Holy Communion frequently. Teach me to embrace the Cross of our crucified Savior as joyfully as you did, so that I may bear my daily burdens with love for Him who suffered for me. Above all, pray that I may avoid sin, live a life of holiness, and attain everlasting salvation.

Amen.

St. Kateri Tekakwitha, pray for us.

RECITE THESE:

Our Father…
Hail Mary…
 Glory Be…

DAY 4 – ST. KATERI TEKAKWITHA

In the name of the Father, and of the Son, and of the Holy Spirit. Amen.

St. Kateri Tekakwitha, beloved child and Lily of the Mohawks, I come before you seeking your intercession for [mention your request here].

I am inspired by the virtues that graced your soul: your deep love for God and neighbor, your humility, obedience, patience, purity, and your spirit of sacrifice. Help me to emulate these virtues in my own life. Through God's abundant grace, which led you to the true faith and holiness, intercede for me and guide me.

DAILY REFLECTION:

Today, reflect on St. Kateri's spirit of sacrifice. She willingly offered her sufferings for the love of Christ and others.

BIBLE PASSAGE: "Greater love has no one than this, that they lay down their life for their friends." - **John 15:13 (GNT)**

Grant me a fervent devotion to the Holy Eucharist, that I may cherish Holy Mass as you did and receive Holy Communion frequently. Teach me to embrace the Cross of our crucified Savior joyfully, as you did, so that I may bear my daily burdens with love for Him who suffered for me. Above all, pray that I may avoid sin, lead a life of holiness, and secure my eternal salvation.

Amen.

St. Kateri Tekakwitha, pray for us.

NOVENA TO ST. KATERI TEKAKWITHA

RECITE THESE:

Our Father…
Hail Mary…
 Glory Be…

DAY 5 – ST. KATERI TEKAKWITHA

In the name of the Father, and of the Son, and of the Holy Spirit. Amen.

St. Kateri Tekakwitha, beloved child and Lily of the Mohawks, I come before you seeking your intercession for [mention your request here].

I am inspired by the virtues that graced your soul: your deep love for God and neighbor, your humility, obedience, patience, purity, and your spirit of sacrifice. Help me to emulate these virtues in my own life. Through God's abundant grace, which led you to the true faith and holiness, intercede for me and guide me.

DAILY REFLECTION:

Today, reflect on St. Kateri's obedience to God's will. Despite challenges, she remained steadfast in following God's path.

BIBLE PASSAGE: "Do everything without complaining or arguing, so that you may become blameless and pure, children of God without fault in a crooked and depraved generation, in which you shine like stars in the universe." - **Philippians 2:14-15 (GNT)**

Grant me a fervent devotion to the Holy Eucharist, that I may cherish Holy Mass as you did and receive Holy Communion frequently. Teach me to embrace the Cross of our crucified Savior joyfully, as you did, so that I may bear my daily crosses with love for Him who suffered for me. Above all, pray that I may avoid sin, lead a holy life, and attain salvation.

Amen.

St. Kateri Tekakwitha, pray for us.

RECITE THESE:

Our Father…
Hail Mary…
 Glory Be…

DAY 6 – ST. KATERI TEKAKWITHA

In the name of the Father, and of the Son, and of the Holy Spirit. Amen.

St. Kateri Tekakwitha, beloved child and Lily of the Mohawks, I come before you seeking your intercession for [mention your request here].

I am inspired by the virtues that graced your soul: your deep love for God and neighbor, your humility, obedience, patience, purity, and your spirit of sacrifice. Help me to emulate these virtues in my own life. Through God's abundant grace, which led you to the true faith and holiness, intercede for me and guide me.

DAILY REFLECTION:

Today, reflect on St. Kateri's purity of heart. She remained steadfast in her commitment to God and lived a life of integrity.

BIBLE PASSAGE: "How can young people keep their lives pure? By obeying your commands." - **Psalm 119:9 (GNT)**

Grant me a fervent devotion to the Holy Eucharist, that I may cherish Holy Mass as you did and receive Holy Communion frequently. Teach me to embrace the Cross of our crucified Savior joyfully, as you did, so that I may bear my daily crosses with love for Him who suffered for me. Above all, pray that I may avoid sin, lead a holy life, and attain eternal salvation.

Amen.

St. Kateri Tekakwitha, pray for us.

RECITE THESE:

Our Father…
Hail Mary…
 Glory Be…

DAY 7 – ST. KATERI TEKAKWITHA

In the name of the Father, and of the Son, and of the Holy Spirit. Amen.

St. Kateri Tekakwitha, beloved child and Lily of the Mohawks, I come before you seeking your intercession for [mention your request here].

I am inspired by the virtues that graced your soul: your deep love for God and neighbor, your humility, obedience, patience, purity, and your spirit of sacrifice. Help me to emulate these virtues in my own life. Through God's abundant grace, which led you to the true faith and holiness, intercede for me and guide me.

DAILY REFLECTION:

Today, reflect on St. Kateri's spirit of sacrifice. She willingly offered her sufferings for the sake of Christ and others.

BIBLE PASSAGE: "For whoever wants to save their life will lose it, but whoever loses their life for me will find it." - **Matthew 16:25 (GNT)**

Grant me a fervent devotion to the Holy Eucharist, that I may cherish Holy Mass as you did and receive Holy Communion frequently. Teach me to embrace the Cross of our crucified Savior joyfully, as you did, so that I may bear my daily crosses with love for Him who suffered for me. Above all, pray that I may avoid sin, lead a life of holiness, and attain eternal salvation.

Amen.

St. Kateri Tekakwitha, pray for us.

NOVENA TO ST. KATERI TEKAKWITHA

RECITE THESE:

Our Father…
Hail Mary…
Glory Be…

DAY 8 – ST. KATERI TEKAKWITHA

In the name of the Father, and of the Son, and of the Holy Spirit. Amen.

St. Kateri Tekakwitha, beloved child and Lily of the Mohawks, I come before you seeking your intercession for [mention your request here].

I am inspired by the virtues that graced your soul: your deep love for God and neighbor, your humility, obedience, patience, purity, and your spirit of sacrifice. Help me to emulate these virtues in my own life. Through God's abundant grace, which led you to the true faith and holiness, intercede for me and guide me.

DAILY REFLECTION:

Today, reflect on St. Kateri's humility. She lived a life of humility, always putting others before herself and giving glory to God.

BIBLE PASSAGE: "But God shows his love for us in that while we were still sinners, Christ died for us." - **Romans 5:8 (GNT)**

Grant me a fervent devotion to the Holy Eucharist, that I may cherish Holy Mass as you did and receive Holy Communion frequently. Teach me to embrace the Cross of our crucified Savior joyfully, as you did, so that I may bear my daily crosses with love for Him who suffered for me. Above all, pray that I may avoid sin, lead a holy life, and attain eternal salvation.

Amen.

St. Kateri Tekakwitha, pray for us.

RECITE THESE:

Our Father…
Hail Mary…
 Glory Be…

DAY 9 – ST. KATERI TEKAKWITHA

In the name of the Father, and of the Son, and of the Holy Spirit. Amen.

St. Kateri Tekakwitha, beloved child and Lily of the Mohawks, I come before you seeking your intercession for [mention your request here].

I am inspired by the virtues that graced your soul: your deep love for God and neighbor, your humility, obedience, patience, purity, and your spirit of sacrifice. Help me to emulate these virtues in my own life. Through God's abundant grace, which led you to the true faith and holiness, intercede for me and guide me.

DAILY REFLECTION:

Today, reflect on St. Kateri's love for the Holy Eucharist. She found great solace and strength in the sacramental presence of Jesus.

BIBLE PASSAGE: "Jesus said to them, 'I am the bread of life. Whoever comes to me will never be hungry, and whoever believes in me will never be thirsty.'" - **John 6:35 (GNT)**

Grant me a fervent devotion to the Holy Eucharist, that I may cherish Holy Mass as you did and receive Holy Communion frequently. Teach me to embrace the Cross of our crucified Savior joyfully, as you did, so that I may bear my daily crosses with love for Him who suffered for me. Above all, pray that I may avoid sin, lead a holy life, and attain eternal salvation.
Amen.

St. Kateri Tekakwitha, pray for us.

NOVENA TO ST. KATERI TEKAKWITHA

RECITE THESE:

Our Father…
Hail Mary…
 Glory Be…

GRATITUDE PRAYER FOR ANSWERED PRAYER

Heavenly Father,

With hearts overflowing with gratitude, we come before you today to thank you for the gift of answered prayer through the intercession of St. Kateri Tekakwitha. Throughout these nine days of prayer, we have poured out our hearts, trusting in your divine providence and the loving intercession of St. Kateri.

You have heard our petitions and granted us your grace and mercy. We thank you for the blessings received, both seen and unseen, knowing that your love for us knows no bounds. Through the example of St. Kateri, you have shown us the power of faith, perseverance, and unwavering trust in your will.

St. Kateri, Lily of the Mohawks, you who knew the challenges of life yet remained steadfast in faith, we are grateful for your heavenly assistance. Your prayers have strengthened us, guided us, and brought us closer to God's loving embrace.

As we reflect on the answered prayers we have received, we commit ourselves anew to living lives of faith, hope, and love. May we emulate St. Kateri's virtues of humility, compassion, and devotion to the Holy Eucharist in all that we do.

We offer this prayer of gratitude in the name of the Father, and of the Son, and of the Holy Spirit. Amen.

St. Kateri Tekakwitha, pray for us.

CONCLUSION

As we conclude this novena to St. Kateri Tekakwitha, we reflect on the journey of faith and prayer we have undertaken together. Over these nine days, we have sought the intercession of St. Kateri, the Lily of the Mohawks, entrusting our needs and intentions to her heavenly care.

Through her example, we have been inspired to deepen our devotion to God, to emulate her virtues of love, humility, and perseverance, and to trust in God's providence in our lives. St. Kateri's life reminds us that no matter the challenges we face, our faith in God can sustain us and lead us to greater holiness.

As we carry forward from this novena, may the prayers we have offered continue to bear fruit in our lives. Let us remain steadfast in prayer, fervent in love for the Holy Eucharist, and compassionate towards all whom we encounter. Let us strive to live as true disciples of Christ, following the path of St. Kateri Tekakwitha with courage and grace.

May St. Kateri Tekakwitha, our heavenly intercessor, continue to guide and bless us, protecting us from harm, and leading us closer to God's eternal love. May her legacy of faith and devotion inspire us always to seek God's will and to live lives of holiness and service.

With hearts full of gratitude for the prayers answered and the blessings received, we conclude this novena in the name of the Father, and of the Son, and of the Holy Spirit. Amen.

St. Kateri Tekakwitha, pray for us.

Made in the USA
Columbia, SC
24 January 2025